A Choice of Cowper's Verse

also by Norman Nicholson

SELECTED POEMS
A LOCAL HABITATION

A Choice of
COWPER'S
Verse

Selected
with an introduction by
NORMAN NICHOLSON

FABER AND FABER
3 Queen Square
London

First published in 1975
by Faber and Faber Limited
3 Queen Square London WC1
Printed in Great Britain by
Latimer Trend & Company Ltd Plymouth
All rights reserved

ISBN 0 571 10633 1 (Faber paperback)
ISBN 0 571 10706 0 (hard bound edition)

Contents

Introduction	*page*	9
On the Receipt of my Mother's Picture		19
From *The Olney Hymns*:		
Walking with God		23
On Opening a Place for Social Prayer		24
Retirement		25
Light Shining out of Darkness		26
The Journey to Emmaus (from *Conversation*)		27
The Watch Fires at Troy		29
(from Homer's *Iliad*, translated)		
Epitaph on a Hare		30
The Snail (translated from Vincent Bourne)		32
To the Nightingale		33
The Colubriad		34
The Retired Cat		36
The Needless Alarm		40
John Gilpin		45
Character of a Prude (from *Truth*)		55
The Flatting Mill		56
Verses Attributed to Alexander Selkirk		57
The Castaway		59
To Mary		62
The Shrubbery		65
The Poplar Field		66
Yardley Oak		67
Extracts from *The Task*		73
Index of First Lines		96

Introduction

William Cowper was born on the 15th November 1731, at Great Berkhamstead Rectory. His father was the son of a judge and the nephew of the first Earl Cowper, while his mother was related to the family of John Donne. It was the mother who was the centre of Cowper's life during his early years at Berkhamstead, and her death, when he was only six, was the first, and perhaps the dominant, tragedy of his life. When she was gone he lost confidence in himself and in the world, and he never really regained it. Throughout his life he seemed to grope towards heaven for a hand to grasp his own, and to turn to his women friends to find one who could take the place of his mother.

This loss was followed by what must have seemed like the loss of his home, for he was sent to a small boarding school about seven miles away at Market Street, where he was bullied and tyrannized until his nervous condition brought on a weakness of the eyes. He was then sent to live with an oculist called Mr. Disney, from whence he went on to Westminster School, where he seems to have been reasonably happy and popular. When, in 'Tirocinium', he revisits his school in memory, his thoughts are admittedly sentimental, but they are those of one who really had been a boy:

> The wall on which we tried our graving skill,
> The very name we carved, subsisting still;
> The bench on which we sat while deep employed,
> Tho' mangled, hacked, and hewed, not yet destroyed:

The little ones, unbuttoned, glowing hot,
Playing our games, and on the very spot;
As happy as we once, to kneel and draw
The chalky ring, and knuckle down at taw;
To pitch the ball into the grounded hat,
Or drive it devious with a dexterous pat.

When he was eighteen Cowper left school and went to live with an attorney in order to study the law. It is obvious that he can never have been fitted for such a profession, but his stay in London was important to him because there he met his cousins, Harriet and Theodora Cowper. Harriet, the elder, who married Sir Thomas Hesketh, was later to be his chief correspondent, and the recipient of some of the most delightful letters in the language; but it was Theodora with whom Cowper fell in love. He was no more fitted to be a lover than to be a barrister, and, though he was inspired to his first attempt at writing verse, it is doubtful if he would ever have faced the problem of marriage. The choice, however, was not left to him, for his uncle, Ashley Cowper, in-sisted that the engagement should be broken off. It was not a harsh decision, for Cowper not only was without sound prospects of a career, he was also showing signs of depression and mental instability. He was assailed by strange fears, which took a religious form, though they probably had their origin in the vicissitudes of his child-hood. He began also to be obsessed by a sense of failure, a sense of being an outcast, singled out from all others for ridicule and shame. About this time his father died, leaving no very large fortune, so that the rest of the family, anxious that Cowper should start to earn his living, used their influence to obtain for him the offer of two administrative posts in the House of Lords. It was, on the face of it, exactly what he had been waiting for, but, in fact, it forced on him the very thing he most wanted to avoid—the need to make a decision. At once he began to imagine the most fantastic objections to the new posts. He could not bring himself to undergo the necessary (formal) examination, and he fancied that he was guilty by desire of the death of the man who held the posts before him. His sense of failure now took the extreme form of belief in his own inevitable damnation, and he wrote those terrible Sapphics after the manner of Isaac Watts:

> Man disavows, and Deity disowns me:
> Hell might afford my miseries a shelter;
> Therefore hell keeps her ever hungry mouths all
> Bolted against me.

He was now clearly out of his mind and there was nowhere for him but an asylum.

Cowper's return to sanity and his conversion to the Evangelical faith were more or less contemporaneous and were obviously interdependent. He had passed slowly from despair through resignation into hope, and then, reading a text in Romans, he felt a sudden inrush of joy and grace. This experience (which was quite characteristic of the religious life of the time) led to the most important phase of his development. His brother John, now a don at Cambridge, found lodgings for him at Huntingdon, where he got to know the Unwins, with whom, after a short while, he went to live. The Unwins were a pious family, typical of the Evangelicals within the Church of England. These Anglican Evangelicals, as a whole, were Calvinist, but more moderate, less Puritanical, than the left-wing of the Revival led by Whitefield. At the same time they were distinguished from the Wesleyans by a much greater retraint, and by a greater regard for the Establishment and for the forms and liturgy of the

Church. They were quite different in temper and outlook from the seventeenth-century Puritans, replacing the old fiery fanaticism by a sweet and gentle glow of faith which is wonderfully caught by Cowper in his description of the journey to Emmaus. It may seem to us that their piety was too highly strung and their cheerfulness too conscientiously consistent for Cowper's delicate and excitable nerves, but there is no doubt that the time he spent with the Unwins was the happiest of his adult life. Moreover it was there that he felt that exaltation, that awakening of the spirit, without which he would never have begun to be a poet.

After the death of Mr. Unwin, his widow took care of Cowper and the two moved to Olney to be near the Reverend John Newton. Newton, a man whose early life had been one of wild adventure and great hardship, was one of the most uncompromising and romantic figures of the Revival. He had little understanding of Cowper and he drove him far too hard, but he showed sympathy and immense patience at a time when such were very much needed. For by now the first fervour of Cowper's faith had subsided, and, in the lassitude of spirit which followed, he began to return to his old obsession with damnation.

It was partly to distract him from those fears that Newton suggested he should write what have now become known as the Olney Hymns. For the most part they are what one might expect—the forced and mechanical expression of a dogma which was more of an anxiety than a comfort; but in just a few of them Cowper captures the spirit of his early conversion and expresses it in words which are part of the folk-poetry of English Protestantism. They may not have quite the broad, almost cosmic, gestures of Watts, nor the searching, probing intimacy of Charles Wesley, but they have a quiet, introspective poignancy which is intensely personal and yet which somehow can be shared by a congregation. 'O for a closer walk with God', 'God moves in a mysterious way', 'There is a fountain filled with blood', and one or two more are achievements of real and lasting value.

But they failed in their primary purpose of distracting Cowper from his melancholy, which increased until, in a dream, he thought that he heard the voice of God speaking his irrevocable doom. There followed another attack of madness, during which he lived for about a year at the Vicarage, and when, eventually, he was well enough to return with Mrs. Unwin to their own house of Orchard Side, he was changed and almost, as one might say, reborn. It was, however, a rebirth which was half a death. The hopes of his youth, the fervour of his conversion, the joy of his first months with the Unwins, were all dead to him for ever. He still subscribed to the formula of the Evangelical faith, and he retained all its humanitarian sympathies and enthusiasms, but it was a faith which seemed to hold no promise for him and pointed only to damnation. He needed, therefore, an interest or a love which would focus his thoughts away from himself, away from his own problems and fears, and he found both interest and love in nature.

At this time the countryside was being rediscovered, the Picturesque was the fashion, and the intellectuals were taking up ruins and romantic scenery as a new hobby. But Cowper was quite untouched by the fashions; indeed, he was scarcely aware of them. He discovered nature not by studying the paintings of Claude Lorraine or the writings of William Gilpin, but by keeping tame hares and digging in his garden. Through these he began to learn of the objective life of nature, to realize that it was not just a gigantic picture-book or even a moral pageant set up for man's benefit. The hedges and fields and streams existed in their own way, and because of this they meant more to him, for they were not involved in his own predicament. For him the next day or night might bring madness or death, but these material things were solid, safe, and comparatively enduring. He clung, therefore, to tree, flower, beast, and bird and even to the stones in the garden wall and the furniture in the parlour, as if they were the only secure things in his world, and he looked at them with love and gratitude and with a most gracious humility.

By this time Newton had left Olney for a parish in London, so that, to occupy his time, Cowper began to write. His first poems—the series of eight Moral Satires —were not very happy in their choice of subject, being largely rather naïve versifications of Calvinist doctrine. Nevertheless, they helped him to exercise his muscles, and, above all, to get into the habit of composing—for poetry, with Cowper, was a matter more of routine than of inspiration. Then, in the summer of 1781, Lady Austen, an attractive and vivacious young widow, visited her sister, who was the wife of a local parson. She at once took a fancy to the poet, who, in spite of his oddness and timidity, had always a strong fascination for women. Almost before he knew what was happening, he was picnicking in Weston Woods, lunching out three days a week, listening to the harpsichord, and even composing a comic ballad ('John Gilpin') which was to be sung all over London. It was a delightful and surprising experience, but it could not go on for ever. Lady Austen was not the sort to do things by half. She could never be satisfied by an ambiguous friendship, and yet anything beyond friendship was impossible for Cowper—besides, his first emotional allegiance went to Mary Unwin, on whom rested his whole hope of health and sanity. So, after a year or two, Lady Austen had to part from him, but not before she had done an immense service both to the poet and to poetry. One day, when he was searching for a subject for a poem in blank verse, she had suggested playfully that he should write about the sofa. And that was the beginning of 'The Task'.

'The Task' provided the ideal medium for Cowper's genius. It is neither didactic nor autobiographical, but discursive. It is slack in tension and low-pitched in tone, and its unity is not of subject nor of form, but rather of personality. It makes some pretence at being an Evangelical sermon, yet Cowper's heart is not in the preaching, but (once he has dutifully dealt with the sofa) in the descriptions of the countryside, the cataloguing of country pleasures, the defence of rural life, and the passionate plea for the care and protection of animals.

There is no need to tell in detail the rest of his life. Much of it was taken up with the translation of Homer, a work which, though heavily Miltonic in language and syntax, is still readable and even, in the case of 'The Odyssey', enjoyable. His most important contribution to literature after 'The Task' lies not in poetry but in the letters, many of which were written to Lady Hesketh, whose friendship brought much pleasure to him in middle age. His final years, however, were of almost unrelieved sorrow. Mrs. Unwin broke down in health and he was left sinking deeper and deeper into the gloom which has its fullest expression in the storm imagery of 'The Castaway'.

Cowper's life was a tragic one, yet it is not for tragedy that we turn to his poems. His poetry, at its best, is the poetry of pleasure, of the plain, ordinary pleasures which every man can enjoy. Again, though Cowper himself was always on the verge of insanity, his poetry is essentially the poetry of the sane. He is in every way a paradox: a recluse who became the spokesman of a great popular religious and democratic movement; and an oddity, an eccentric, a refugee from society, who, perhaps more than any other English poet, expressed the aspirations of the average man of his time. His poetry is rarely exciting, rarely adventurous in language or form, yet it has passages of unaffected felicity which are memorable and moving. It does not try to reveal the unseen, but it makes things seen appear with a new and astonishing clarity.

In his response to the emotional appeal of the Revival and in his awareness of the environment of man, Cowper was one of the forerunners of the Romantic Movement. Yet he was, at the same time, a man of the eighteenth century. He rejected its morality and social code; he rejected its hedonism and materialism; he rejected its urban way of life and its worldly values—but he approved of its good sense and courtesy, and in spite of his love of solitude, he approved of its sociableness. His poetry has all the merits which its age demanded from good conversation—it is never obscure nor embarrassingly private; it always presumes an audience and adjusts itself to that audience. It is this quality which helps to make him one of the most successful writers of light verse. Poems like 'The Colubriad' may not have the wit of Pope nor the dexterity of Prior, but they have an unforced humour, an intuitive tact in the telling, which make them quite as effective in their own way.

Yet, though Cowper rarely parades his sorrow in his poetry the sorrow was still there:

> I was a stricken deer, that left the herd
> Long since; with many an arrow deep infixt
> My panting side was charged, when I withdrew
> To seek a tranquil death in distant shades.
> There I was found by one who had himself

Been hurt by the archers. In his side he bore,
And in his hands and feet, the cruel scars.
With gentle force soliciting the darts,
He drew them forth, and healed, and bade me live.
Since then, with few associates, in remote
And silent woods I wander, far from those
My former partners of the peopled scene.

'The Task', Book III

Once read, the tone of those lines can never be forgotten. We hear it always in Cowper's voice, whether he is describing the chickens in the snow or the tea-urn by the fire. Every sight and sound was doubly dear and seen doubly clear because he feared he might never see it again. He looked his last on all things lovely every hour. He was walking always between the joy and brightness of the transient and the terror and darkness of the eternal. We may feel, as surely we must feel, that his terrors were without cause, yet we cannot but admire the courage with which he faced them. It is this courage which gives a true dignity to a life which might otherwise have seemed full of trivial things. In his letters we see that, so long as he retained his sanity, he never lost his love and concern for his fellow men. 'Through the loopholes of retreat' he could send a noble and not ignored challenge to the slave-owners, and to all who oppressed or exploited any living creature. In the letters, too, we see his imagination and humour playing like firelight over everyday affairs (the escape of a tame hare, the warping of a table-leg, the ordering of a hat, an unexplained knock on the door), till they form a personal landscape which is neither insignificant nor dull. The letters, because they are so spontaneous, so unpretentious, are perhaps more nearly perfect than the poems, but it is in the poems that we find the full clarity of Cowper's vision of nature. It was a vision unlike anything which had come before it in English literature: he saw things as they are, but in the sad, yellow brightness of a sun that was always on the point of setting.

NORMAN NICHOLSON

On the Receipt of my Mother's Picture
Out of Norfolk

Oh that those lips had language! Life has passed
With me but roughly since I heard thee last.
Those lips are thine—thy own sweet smiles I see,
The same that oft in childhood solaced me;
Voice only fails, else how distinct they say,
'Grieve not, my child, chase all thy fears away!'
The meek intelligence of those dear eyes
(Blest be the Art that can immortalize,—
The Art that baffles Time's tyrannic claim
To quench it) here shines on me still the same.
    Faithful remembrancer of one so dear,
O welcome guest, though unexpected, here!
Who bidst me honour with an artless song,
Affectionate, a mother lost so long.
I will obey, not willingly alone,
But gladly, as the precept were her own:
And while that face renews my filial grief,
Fancy shall weave a charm for my relief,—
Shall steep me in Elysian reverie,
A momentary dream, that thou art she.
    My mother! when I learned that thou wast dead,
Say, wast thou conscious of the tears I shed?
Hovered thy spirit o'er thy sorrowing son,
Wretch even then, life's journey just begun?
Perhaps thou gavest me, though unseen, a kiss;
Perhaps a tear, if souls can weep in bliss—
Ah, that maternal smile! it answers—'Yes.'

I heard the bell tolled on thy burial day,
I saw the hearse that bore the slow away,
And, turning from my nursery window, drew
A long, long sigh, and wept a last adieu!
But was it such?—It was.—Where thou art gone
Adieus and farewells are a sound unknown;
May I but meet thee on that peaceful shore,
The parting sound shall pass my lips no more!
Thy maidens grieved themselves at my concern,
Oft gave me promise of a quick return.
What ardently I wished, I long believed,
And, disappointed still, was still deceived;
By disappointment every day beguiled,
Dupe of to-morrow even from a child.
Thus many a sad to-morrow came and went,
Till, all my stock of infant sorrow spent,
I learned at last submission to my lot,
But, though I less deplored thee, ne'er forgot.

Where once we dwelt our name is heard no more,
Children not thine have trod my nursery floor;
And where the gardener Robin, day by day,
Drew me to school along the public way,
Delighted with my bauble coach, and wrapped
In scarlet mantle warm, and velvet capped,
'Tis now become a history little known,
That once we called the pastoral house our own.
Shortlived possession! but the record fair,
That memory keeps of all thy kindness there,
Still outlives many a storm that has effaced
A thousand other themes less deeply traced.
Thy nightly visits to my chamber made,
That thou mightest know me safe and warmly laid;
Thy morning bounties ere I left my home,
The biscuit, or confectionary plum;
The fragrant waters on my cheeks bestowed

By thy own hand, till fresh they shone and glowed:
All this, and more endearing still than all,
Thy constant flow of love, that knew no fall,
Ne'er roughened by those cataracts and breaks,
That humour interposed too often makes;
All this still legible in Memory's page,
And still to be so to my latest age,
Adds joy to duty, makes me glad to pay
Such honours to thee as my numbers may;
Perhaps a frail memorial, but sincere,
Not scorned in Heaven, though little noticed here.

Could Time, his flight reversed, restore the hours
When playing with thy vesture's tissued flowers,
The violet, the pink, and jessamine,
I pricked them into paper with a pin,
(And thou wast happier than myself the while,
Wouldst softly speak, and stroke my head and smile),
Could those few pleasant hours again appear,
Might one wish bring them, would I wish them here?
I would not trust my heart—the dear delight
Seems so to be desired, perhaps I might.—
But no—what here we call our life is such,
So little to be loved, and thou so much,
That I should ill requite thee, to constrain
Thy unbound spirit into bonds again.

Thou, as a gallant bark from Albion's coast
(The storms all weathered and the ocean crossed)
Shoots into port at some well-havened isle,
Where spices breathe, and brighter seasons smile,
There sits quiescent on the floods that show
Her beauteous form reflected clear below,
While airs impregnated with incense play
Around her, fanning light her streamers gay;—
So thou, with sails how swift! has reached the shore,
'Where tempests never beat nor billows roar;'

And thy loved consort on the dangerous tide
Of life, long since has anchored at thy side.
But me, scarce hoping to attain that rest,
Always from port withheld, always distressed—
Me howling blasts drive devious, tempest-tossed,
Sails ripped, seams opening wide, and compass lost,
And day by day some current's thwarting force
Sets me more distant from a prosperous course.
But oh the thought, that thou art safe, and he!
That thought is joy, arrive what may to me.
My boast is not that I deduce my birth
From loins enthroned, and rulers of the earth;
But higher far my proud pretensions rise—
The son of parents passed into the skies.
And now, Farewell.—Time unrevoked has run
His wonted course, yet what I wished is done.
By Contemplation's help, not sought in vain,
I seem to have lived my childhood o'er again;
To have renewed the joys that once were mine,
Without the sin of violating thine;
And while the wings of Fancy still are free,
And I can view this mimic show of thee,
Time has but half succeeded in his theft—
Thyself removed, thy power to soothe me left.

Walking with God
Gen. v. 24

Oh! for a closer walk with God,
  A calm and heavenly frame;
A light to shine upon the road
  That leads me to the Lamb!

Where is the blessedness I knew
  When first I saw the Lord?
Where is the soul-refreshing view
  Of Jesus and his word?

What peaceful hours I once enjoyed!
  How sweet their memory still!
But they have left an aching void,
  The world can never fill.

Return, O holy Dove, return!
  Sweet messenger of rest:
I hate the sins that made thee mourn,
  And drove thee from my breast.

The dearest idol I have known,
  Whate'er that idol be,
Help me to tear it from thy throne,
  And worship only thee.

So shall my walk be close with God,
  Calm and serene my frame;
So purer light shall mark the road
  That leads me to the Lamb.

On Opening a Place for Social Prayer

Jesus, where'er thy people meet,
There they behold thy mercy-seat;
Where'er they seek thee thou art found,
And ev'ry place is hallow'd ground.

For thou, within no walls confin'd,
Inhabitest the humble mind;
Such ever bring thee, where they come,
And going, take thee to their home.

Dear Shepherd of thy chosen few!
Thy former mercies here renew;
Here, to our waiting hearts, proclaim
The sweetness of thy saving name.

Here may we prove the pow'r of pray'r,
To strengthen faith, and sweeten care;
To teach our faint desires to rise,
And bring all heav'n before our eyes.

Behold! at thy commanding word,
We stretch the curtain and the cord;
Come thou, and fill this wider space,
And help us with a large encrease.

Lord, we are few, but thou art near;
Nor short thine arm, nor deaf thine ear;
Oh rend the heav'ns, come quickly down,
And make a thousand hearts thine own!

Retirement

Far from the world, O Lord, I flee,
  From strife and tumult far;
From scenes, where Satan wages still
  His most successful war.

The calm retreat, the silent shade,
  With pray'r and praise agree;
And seem by thy sweet bounty made,
  For those who follow thee.

There if thy Spirit touch the soul,
  And grace her mean abode;
Oh with what peace, and joy, and love,
  She communes with her God!

There like the nightingale she pours
  Her solitary lays;
Nor asks a witness of her song,
  Nor thirsts for human praise.

Author and Guardian of my life,
  Sweet source of light divine;
And (all harmonious names in one)
  My Saviour; thou art mine!

What thanks I owe thee, and what love
  A boundless, endless store;
Shall echo thro' the realms above,
  When time shall be no more.

Light Shining out of Darkness

God moves in a mysterious way
   His wonders to perform;
He plants his footsteps in the sea,
   And rides upon the storm.

Deep in unfathomable mines
   Of never-failing skill,
He treasures up his bright designs
   And works his sovereign will.

Ye fearful saints, fresh courage take,
   The clouds ye so much dread
Are big with mercy, and shall break
   In blessings on your head.

Judge not the Lord by feeble sense,
   But trust him for his grace:
Behind a frowning providence
   He hides a smiling face.

His purposes will ripen fast,
   Unfolding every hour;
The bud may have a bitter taste,
   But sweet will be the flower.

Blind unbelief is sure to err,
   And scan his work in vain:
God is his own interpreter,
   And he will make it plain.

The Journey to Emmaus

It happened on a solemn eventide,
Soon after he that was our surety died,
Two bosom friends, each pensively inclined,
The scene of all those sorrows left behind,
Sought their own village, busied as they went
In musings worthy of the great event:
They spake of him they loved, of him whose life,
Though blameless, had incurred perpetual strife,
Whose deeds had left, in spite of hostile arts,
A deep memorial graven on their hearts.
The recollection, like a vein of ore,
The farther traced, enriched them still the more;
They thought him, and they justly thought him, one
Sent to do more than he appeared to have done;
To exalt a people, and to place them high
Above all else, and wondered he should die.
Ere yet they brought their journey to an end,
A stranger joined them, courteous as a friend,
And asked them, with a kind, engaging air,
What their affliction was, and begged a share.
Informed, he gathered up the broken thread,
And, Truth and Wisdom gracing all he said,
Explained, illustrated, and searched so well
The tender theme on which they chose to dwell,
That, reaching home, 'The night,' they said, 'is near,
We must not now be parted, sojourn here.'
The new acquaintance soon became a guest,
And made so welcome at their simple feast,
He blessed the bread, but vanished at the word,

And left them both exclaiming, ' 'Twas the Lord!
Did not our hearts feel all he deigned to say,
Did they not burn within us by the way?'

From CONVERSATION

The Watch Fires at Troy

Big with great purposes and proud they sat,
Not disarrayed, but in fair form disposed
Of even ranks, and watched their numerous fires.
As when around the clear bright moon, the stars
Shine in full splendour, and the winds are hushed,
The groves, the mountain-tops, the headland-heights
Stand all apparent, not a vapour streaks
The boundless blue, but ether opened wide
All glitters, and the shepherd's heart is cheered;
So numerous seemed those fires the bank between
Of Xanthus, blazing, and the fleet of Greece,
In prospect all of Troy; a thousand fires,
Each watched by fifty warriors seated near.
The steeds beside the chariots stood, their corn
Chewing, and waiting till the golden-throned
Aurora should restore the light of day.

Translated from Homer's ILIAD, BOOK VIII

Epitaph on a Hare

Here lies, whom hound did ne'er pursue,
  Nor swifter greyhound follow,
Whose foot ne'er tainted morning dew,
  Nor ear heard huntsman's halloo;

Old Tiny, surliest of his kind,
  Who, nursed, with tender care,
And to domestic bounds confined,
  Was still a wild Jack hare.

Though duly from my hand he took
  His pittance every night,
He did it with a jealous look,
  And, when he could, would bite.

His diet was of wheaten bread,
  And milk, and oats, and straw;
Thistles, or lettuces instead,
  With sand to scour his maw.

On twigs of hawthorn he regaled,
  On pippins' russet peel,
And when his juicy salads failed,
  Sliced carrot pleased him well.

A Turkey carpet was his lawn,
  Whereon he loved to bound,
To skip and gambol like a fawn,
  And swing his rump around.

His frisking was at evening hours,
    For then he lost his fear,
But most before approaching showers,
    Or when a storm drew near.

Eight years and five round-rolling moons
    He thus saw steal away,
Dozing out all his idle noons,
    And every night at play.

I kept him for his humour's sake,
    For he would oft beguile
My heart of thoughts that made it ache,
    And force me to a smile.

But now, beneath this walnut shade,
    He finds his long, last home,
And waits, in snug concealment laid,
    Till gentler Puss shall come.

He, still more aged, feels the shocks,
    From which no care can save,
And partner once of Tiny's box,
    Must soon partake his grave.

The Snail

To grass, or leaf, or fruit, or wall,
The snail sticks close, nor fears to fall,
As if he grew there, house and all
                Together.

Within that house secure he hides,
When danger imminent betides
Of storm, or other harm besides
                Of weather.

Give but his horns the slightest touch,
His self-collecting power is such
He shrinks into his house, with much
                Displeasure.

Where'er he dwells, he dwells alone,
Except himself has chattels none,
Well satisfied to be his own
                Whole treasure.

Thus, hermit-like, his life he leads,
Nor partner of his banquet needs,
And if he meets one, only feeds
                The faster.

Who seeks him must be worse than blind,
(He and his house are so combin'd)
If, finding it, he fails to find
                Its master.

Translated from VINCENT BOURNE

To the Nightingale

WHICH THE AUTHOR HEARD SUNG ON NEW
YEAR'S DAY, 1792

Whence is it, that amaz'd I hear
　From yonder wither'd spray,
This foremost morn of all the year,
　The melody of May?

And why, since thousands would be proud
　Of such a favour shewn,
Am I selected from the crowd,
　To witness it alone?

Sing'st thou, sweet Philomel, to me,
　For that I also long
Have practis'd in the groves like thee,
　Though not like thee in song?

Or sing'st thou rather under force
　Of some divine command,
Commission'd to presage a course
　Of happier days at hand?

Thrice welcome then! for many a long
　And joyless year have I
As thou to-day, put forth my song
　Beneath a wintry sky.

But thee no wintry skies can harm,
　Who only need'st to sing,
To make ev'n January charm,
　And ev'ry season Spring.

The Colubriad

Close by the threshold of a door nailed fast
Three kittens sat; each kitten looked aghast.
I, passing swift and inattentive by,
At the three kittens cast a careless eye;
Not much concerned to know what they did there,
Not deeming kittens worth a poet's care.
But presently a loud and furious hiss
Caused me to stop, and to exclaim, 'What's this?'
When lo! upon the threshold met my view,
With head erect, and eyes of fiery hue,
A viper, long as Count de Grasse's queue.
Forth from his head his forked tongue he throws,
Darting it full against a kitten's nose;
Who having never seen, in field or house,
The like, sat still and silent as a mouse;
Only projecting, with attention due,
Her whiskered face, she asked him, 'Who are you?'
On to the hall went I, with pace not slow,
But swift as lightning, for a long Dutch hoe;
With which well armed I hastened to the spot,
To find the viper, but I found him not.
And turning up the leaves and shrubs around,
Found only that he was not to be found.
But still the kittens, sitting as before,
Sat watching close the bottom of the door.
'I hope,' said I, 'the villain I would kill
Has slipped between the door and the door's sill;
And if I make dispatch, and follow hard,
No doubt but I shall find him in the yard:'

For long ere now it should have been rehearsed,
'Twas in the garden that I found him first.
E'en there I found him, there the full-grown cat
His head, with velvet paw, did gently pat:
As curious as the kittens erst had been
To learn what this phenomenon might mean.
Filled with heroic ardour at the sight,
And fearing every moment he would bite,
And rob our household of our only cat
That was of age to combat with a rat;
With outstretched hoe I slew him at the door,
And taught him NEVER TO COME THERE NO MORE.

The Retired Cat

A poet's cat, sedate and grave
As poet well could wish to have,
Was much addicted to inquire
For nooks to which she might retire,
And where, secure as mouse in chink,
She might repose, or sit and think.
I know not where she caught the trick—
   Nature perhaps herself had cast her
In such a mould philosophique,
   Or else she learned it of her master.
Sometimes ascending, debonair,
An apple tree, or lofty pear,
Lodged with convenience in the fork,
She watched the gardener at his work;
Sometimes her ease and solace sought
In an old empty watering-pot;
There, wanting nothing save a fan,
To seem some nymph in her sedan
Apparelled in exactest sort,
And ready to be borne to court.
   But love of change, it seems, has place,
Not only in our wiser race;
Cats also feel, as well as we,
That passion's force, and so did she.
Her climbing, she began to find,
Exposed her too much to the wind,
And the old utensil of tin
Was cold and comfortless within:
She therefore wished instead of those

Some place of more serene repose,
Where neither cold might come, nor air
Too rudely wanton with her hair,
And sought it in the likeliest mode
Within her master's snug abode.
   A drawer, it chanced, at bottom lined
With linen of the softest kind,
With such as merchants introduce
From India, for the ladies' use,
A drawer impending o'er the rest
Half open in the topmost chest,
Of depth enough, and none to spare,
Invited her to slumber there;
Puss with delight beyond expression
Surveyed the scene, and took possession.
Recumbent at her ease, ere long,
And lulled by her own humdrum song,
She left the cares of life behind,
   And slept as she would sleep her last,
When in came, housewifely inclined,
   The chambermaid, and shut it fast;
But no malignity impelled,
But all unconscious whom it held.
   Awakened by the shock (cried Puss)
'Was ever cat attended thus?
The open drawer was left, I see,
Merely to prove a nest for me,
For soon as I was well composed,
Then came the maid, and it was closed,
How smooth these 'kerchiefs, and how sweet!
Oh what a delicate retreat!
I will resign myself to rest
Till Sol, declining in the west,
Shall call to supper, when, no doubt,
Susan will come and let me out.'

The evening came, the sun descended,
And Puss remained still unattended.
The night rolled tardily away,
(With her indeed 'twas never day),
The sprightly morn her course renewed,
The evening gray again ensued,
And puss came into mind no more
Than if entombed the day before.
With hunger pinched, and pinched for room,
She now presaged approaching doom,
Nor slept a single wink, or purred,
Conscious of jeopardy incurred.

That night, by chance, the poet watching,
Heard an inexplicable scratching;
His noble heart went pit-a-pat,
And to himself he said—'What's that?'
He drew the curtain at his side,
And forth he peeped, but nothing spied.
Yet, by his ear directed, guessed
Something imprisoned in the chest,
And, doubtful what, with prudent care
Resolved it should continue there.
At length a voice which well he knew,
A long and melancholy mew,
Saluting his poetic ears,
Consoled him and dispelled his fears:
He left his bed, he trod the floor,
He 'gan in haste the drawers explore,
The lowest first, and without stop
The rest in order to the top.
For 'tis a truth well known to most,
That whatsoever thing is lost,
We seek it, ere it come to light,
In every cranny but the right.
Forth skipped the cat, not now replete

As erst with airy self-conceit,
Nor in her own fond apprehension
A theme for all the world's attention,
But modest, sober, cured of all
Her notions hyperbolical,
And wishing for a place of rest
Any thing rather than a chest.
Then stepped the poet into bed,
With this reflection in his head.

MORAL

Beware of too sublime a sense
Of your own worth and consequence:
The man who dreams himself so great
And his importance of such weight,
That all around, in all that's done,
Must move and act for him alone,
Will learn in school of tribulation
The folly of his expectation.

The Needless Alarm

A TALE

There is a field through which I often pass,
Thick overspread with moss and silky grass,
Adjoining close to Kilwick's echoing wood,
Where oft the bitch-fox hides her hapless brood,
Reserv'd to solace many a neighb'ring squire,
That he may follow them through brake and briar,
Contusion hazarding of neck or spine,
Which rural gentlemen call sport divine.
A narrow brook by rushy banks conceal'd,
Runs in a bottom, and divides the field;
Oaks intersperse it, that had once a head,
But now wear crests of oven-wood instead;
And where the land slopes to its wat'ry bourn,
Wide yawns a gulph beside a ragged thorn;
Bricks line the sides, but shiver'd long ago,
And horrid brambles intertwine below;
A hollow scoop'd, I judge, in ancient time,
For baking earth, or burning rock to lime.

Not yet the hawthorn bore her berries red,
With which the fieldfare, wint'ry guest, is fed;
Nor autumn yet had brush'd from ev'ry spray,
With her chill hand, the mellow leaves away;
But corn was hous'd, and beans were in the stack,
Now, therefore, issued forth the spotted pack,
With tails high mounted, ears hung low, and throats
With a whole gamut fill'd of heav'nly notes,
For which, alas! my destiny severe,
Though ears she gave me two, gave me no ear.

The sun, accomplishing his early march,
His lamp now planted on heav'n's topmost arch,
When, exercise and air my only aim,
And heedless whither, to that field I came,
Ere yet with ruthless joy the happy hound
Told hill and dale that Reynard's track was found,
Or with the high-rais'd horn's melodious clang
All Kilwick and all Dingle-derry rang.

Sheep graz'd the field; some with soft bosom press'd
The herb as soft, while nibbling stray'd the rest;
Nor noise was heard but of the hasty brook,
Struggling, detain'd in many a petty nook.
All seem'd so peaceful, that from them convey'd
To me, their peace by kind contagion spread.

But when the huntsman, with distended cheek,
'Gan make his instrument of music speak,
And from within the wood that crash was heard,
Though not a hound from whom it burst appear'd,
The sheep recumbent, and the sheep that graz'd,
All huddling into phalanx, stood and gaz'd,
Admiring, terrified, the novel strain,
Then cours'd the field around, and cours'd it round again:
But, recollecting with a sudden thought,
That flight in circles urg'd advanc'd them nought,
They gather'd close around the old pit's brink,
And thought again—but knew not what to think.

The man to solitude accustom'd long
Perceives in ev'ry thing that lives a tongue;
Not animals alone, but shrubs and trees,
Have speech for him, and understood with ease;
After long drought, when rains abundant fall,
He hears the herbs and flow'rs rejoicing all;
Knows what the freshness of their hue implies,
How glad they catch the largess of the skies;
But, with precision nicer still, the mind

He scans of ev'ry loco-motive kind;
Birds of all feather, beasts of ev'ry name,
That serve mankind, or shun them, wild or tame;
The looks and gestures of their griefs and fears
Have, all, articulation in his ears;
He spells them true by intuition's light,
And needs no glossary to set him right.

This truth premis'd was needful as a text,
To win due credence to what follows next.

Awhile they mus'd; surveying ev'ry face,
Thou hadst suppos'd them of superior race;
Their periwigs of wool, and fears combin'd,
Stamp'd on each countenance such marks of mind
That sage they seem'd as lawyers o'er a doubt,
Which, puzzling long, at last they puzzle out;
Or academic tutors, teaching youths,
Sure ne'er to want them, mathematic truths;
When thus a mutton, statelier than the rest,
A ram, the ewes and wethers, sad, address'd:

Friends! we have liv'd too long. I never heard
Sounds such as these, so worthy to be fear'd.
Could I believe, that winds for ages pent
In earth's dark womb have found at last a vent,
And from their prison-house below arise,
With all these hideous howlings to the skies,
I could be much compos'd, nor should appear
For such a cause to feel the slightest fear.
Yourselves have seen, what time the thunders roll'd
All night, me resting quiet in the fold.
Or heard we that tremendous bray alone,
I could expound the melancholy tone;
Should deem it by our old companion made,
The ass; for he, we know, has lately stray'd,
And being lost, perhaps, and wand'ring wide,
Might be suppos'd to clamour for a guide.

But ah! those dreadful yells what soul can hear,
That owns a carcase, and not quake for fear?
Daemons produce them doubtless, brazen-claw'd
And fang'd with brass the daemons are abroad;
I hold it, therefore, wisest and most fit,
That, life to save, we leap into the pit.

　　Him answer'd then his loving mate and true,
But more discreet than he, a Cambrian ewe.

　　How? leap into the pit our life to save?
To save our life leap all into the grave?
For can we find it less? Contemplate first
The depth how awful! falling there we burst;
Or should the brambles, interpos'd, our fall
In part abate, that happiness were small;
For with a race like theirs no chance I see
Of peace or ease to creatures clad as we.
Meantime, noise kills not. Be it Dapple's bray,
Or be it not, or be it whose it may,
And rush those other sounds, that seem by tongues
Of daemons utter'd, from whatever lungs,
Sounds are but sounds, and till the cause appear,
We have at least commodious standing here;
Come, fiend, come, fury, giant, monster, blast
From earth or hell, we can but plunge at last.

　　While thus she spake, I fainter heard the peals,
For Reynard, close attended at his heels,
By panting dog, tir'd man, and spatter'd horse,
Through mere good fortune, took a diff'rent course.
The flock grew calm again, and I, the road
Following that led me to my own abode,
Much wonder'd that the silly sheep had found
Such cause of terror in an empty sound,
So sweet to huntsman, gentleman, and hound.

MORAL

Beware of desp'rate steps. The darkest day
(Live till to-morrow) will have pass'd away.

The Diverting History of John Gilpin

John Gilpin was a citizen
  Of credit and renown,
A train-band captain eke was he
  Of famous London town.

John Gilpin's spouse said to her dear—
  Though wedded we have been
These twice ten tedious years, yet we
  No holiday have seen.

Tomorrow is our wedding-day,
  And we will then repair
Unto the Bell at Edmonton
  All in a chaise and pair.

My sister, and my sister's child,
  Myself, and children three,
Will fill the chaise; so you must ride
  On horseback after we.

He soon replied—I do admire
  Of womankind but one,
And you are she, my dearest dear,
  Therefore it shall be done.

I am a linen-draper bold,
    As all the world doth know,
And my good friend the calender
    Will lend his horse to go.

Quoth Mrs. Gilpin—That's well said;
    And, for that wine is dear,
We will be furnish'd with our own,
    Which is both bright and clear.

John Gilpin kiss'd his loving wife;
    O'erjoy'd was he to find
That, though on pleasure she was bent,
    She had a frugal mind.

The morning came, the chaise was brought,
    But yet was not allow'd
To drive up to the door, lest all
    Should say that she was proud.

So three doors off the chaise was stay'd,
    Where they did all get in;
Six precious souls, and all agog
    To dash through thick and thin!

Smack went the whip, round went the wheels,
    Were never folk so glad,
The stones did rattle underneath,
    As if Cheapside were mad.

John Gilpin at his horse's side
    Seiz'd fast the flowing mane,
And up he got, in haste to ride,
    But soon came down again;

For saddle-tree scarce reach'd had he,
   His journey to begin,
When, turning round his head, he saw
   Three customers come in.

So down he came; for loss of time,
   Although it griev'd him sore,
Yet loss of pence, full well he knew,
   Would trouble him much more.

'Twas long before the customers
   Were suited to their mind,
When Betty screaming came down stairs—
   'The wine is left behind!'

Good lack! quoth he—yet bring it me,
   My leathern belt likewise,
In which I bear my trusty sword
   When I do exercise.

Now mistress Gilpin (careful soul!)
   Had two stone bottles found,
To hold the liquor that she lov'd,
   And keep it safe and sound.

Each bottle had a curling ear,
   Through which the belt he drew,
And hung a bottle on each side,
   To make his balance true.

Then, over all, that he might be
   Equipp'd from top to toe,
His long red cloak, well brush'd and neat,
   He manfully did throw.

Now see him mounted once again
   Upon his nimble steed,
Full slowly pacing o'er the stones,
   With caution and good heed!

But, finding soon a smoother road
   Beneath his well-shod feet,
The snorting beast began to trot,
   Which gall'd him in his seat.

So, Fair and softly, John he cried,
   But John he cried in vain;
That trot became a gallop soon,
   In spite of curb and rein.

So stooping down, as needs he must
   Who cannot sit upright,
He grasp'd the mane with both his hands,
   And eke with all his might.

His horse, who never in that sort
   Had handled been before,
What thing upon his back had got
   Did wonder more and more.

Away went Gilpin, neck or nought;
   Away went hat and wig!—
He little dreamt, when he set out,
   Of running such a rig!

The wind did blow, the cloak did fly,
   Like streamer long and gay,
Till, loop and button failing both,
   At last it flew away.

Then might all people well discern
   The bottles he had slung;
A bottle swinging at each side,
   As hath been said or sung.

The dogs did bark, the children scream'd,
   Up flew the windows all;
And ev'ry soul cried out—Well done!
   As loud as he could bawl.

Away went Gilpin—who but he?
   His fame soon spread around—
He carries weight! he rides a race!
   'Tis for a thousand pound!

And still, as fast as he drew near,
   'Twas wonderful to view
How in a trice the turnpike-men
   Their gates wide open threw.

And now, as he went bowing down
   His reeking head full low,
The bottles twain behind his back
   Were shatter'd at a blow.

Down ran the wine into the road,
   Most piteous to be seen,
Which made his horse's flanks to smoke
   As they had basted been.

But still he seem'd to carry weight,
   With leathern girdle brac'd;
For all might see the bottle-necks
   Still dangling at his waist.

Thus all through merry Islington
　　These gambols he did play,
And till he came unto the Wash
　　Of Edmonton so gay.

And there he threw the wash about
　　On both sides of the way,
Just like unto a trundling mop,
　　Or a wild goose at play.

At Edmonton his loving wife
　　From the balcony spied
Her tender husband, wond'ring much
　　To see how he did ride.

Stop, stop, John Gilpin!—Here's the house—
　　They all at once did cry;
The dinner waits, and we are tir'd:
　　Said Gilpin—So am I!

But yet his horse was not a whit
　　Inclin'd to tarry there;
For why?—his owner had a house
　　Full ten miles off, at Ware.

So like an arrow swift he flew,
　　Shot by an archer strong;
So did he fly—which brings me to
　　The middle of my song.

Away went Gilpin, out of breath,
　　And sore against his will,
Till at his friend the calender's
　　His horse at last stood still.

The calender, amaz'd to see
    His neighbour in such trim,
Laid down his pipe, flew to the gate,
    And thus accosted him:—

What news? what news? your tidings tell;
    Tell me you must and shall—
Say why bare-headed you are come,
    Or why you come at all?

Now Gilpin had a pleasant wit,
    And lov'd a timely joke;
And thus unto the calender
    In merry guise he spoke:—

I came because your horse would come;
    And, if I well forbode,
My hat and wig will soon be here—
    They are upon the road.

The calender, right glad to find
    His friend in merry pin,
Return'd him not a single word,
    But to the house went in;

Whence straight he came with hat and wig;
    A wig that flow'd behind,
A hat not much the worse for wear,
    Each comely in its kind.

He held them up, and, in his turn,
    Thus show'd his ready wit—
My head is twice as big as your's,
    They therefore needs must fit.

But let me scrape the dirt away
    That hangs upon your face;
And stop and eat, for well you may
    Be in a hungry case.

Said John—It is my wedding-day,
    And all the world would stare,
If wife should dine at Edmonton
    And I should dine at Ware!

So, turning to his horse, he said—
    I am in haste to dine;
'Twas for your pleasure you came here,
    You shall go back for mine.

Ah, luckless speech, and bootless boast!
    For which he paid full dear;
For, while he spake, a braying ass
    Did sing most loud and clear;

Whereat his horse did snort, as he
    Had heard a lion roar,
And gallop'd off with all his might,
    As he had done before.

Away went Gilpin, and away
    Went Gilpin's hat and wig!
He lost them sooner than at first—
    For why?—they were too big!

Now, mistress Gilpin, when she saw
    Her husband posting down
Into the country far away,
    She pull'd out half a crown;

And thus unto the youth she said
  That drove them to the Bell—
This shall be yours when you bring back
  My husband safe and well.

The youth did ride, and soon did meet
  John coming back amain;
Whom in a trice he tried to stop,
  By catching at his rein;

But, not performing what he meant,
  And gladly would have done,
The frighted steed he frighted more,
  And made him faster run.

Away went Gilpin, and away
  Went post-boy at his heels!—
The post-boy's horse right glad to miss
  The lumb'ring of the wheels.

Six gentlemen upon the road,
  Thus seeing Gilpin fly,
With post-boy scamp'ring in the rear,
  They rais'd the hue and cry:

Stop thief! stop thief!—a highwayman!
  Not one of them was mute;
And all and each that pass'd that way
  Did join in the pursuit.

And now the turnpike gates again
  Flew open in short space;
The toll-men thinking, as before,
  That Gilpin rode a race.

And so he did—and won it too!—
    For he got first to town;
Nor stopp'd till where he had got up
    He did again get down.

Now let us sing—Long live the king,
    And Gilpin long live he;
And, when he next doth ride abroad,
    May I be there to see!

Character of a Prude

Yon ancient prude, whose withered features show
She might be young some forty years ago,
Her elbows pinioned close upon her hips,
Her head erect, her fan upon her lips,
Her eyebrows arched, her eyes both gone astray
To watch yon amorous couple in their play,
With bony and unkerchiefed neck defies
The rude inclemency of wintry skies,
And sails with lappet head and mincing airs,
Duly at clink of bell to morning prayers.
To thrift and parsimony much inclined,
She yet allows herself that boy behind;
The shivering urchin, bending as he goes,
With slipshod heels, and dewdrop at his nose,
His predecessor's coat advanced to wear,
Which future pages yet are doomed to share,
Carries her Bible tucked beneath his arm,
And hides his hands to keep his fingers warm.

From TRUTH

The Flatting Mill

When a bar of pure silver or ingot of gold
Is sent to be flatted or wrought into length,
It is passed between cylinders often, and rolled
In an engine of utmost mechanical strength.

Thus tortured and squeezed, at last it appears
Like a loose heap of ribbon, a glittering show,
Like music it tinkles and rings in your ears,
And, warmed by the pressure, is all in a glow.

This process achieved, it is doomed to sustain
The thump after thump of a gold-beater's mallet,
And at last is of service in sickness or pain
To cover a pill for a delicate palate.

Alas for the poet! who dares undertake
To urge reformation of national ill—
His head and his heart are both likely to ache
With the double employment of mallet and mill.

If he wish to instruct, he must learn to delight,
Smooth, ductile, and even his fancy must flow,
Must tinkle and glitter like gold to the sight,
And catch in its progress a sensible glow.

After all he must beat it as thin and as fine
As the leaf that enfolds what an invalid swallows;
For truth is unwelcome, however divine,
And unless you adorn it, a nausea follows.

Verses

Supposed to be written by Alexander Selkirk, during his solitary abode in the island of Juan Fernandez

I am monarch of all I survey,
  My right there is none to dispute,
From the centre all round to the sea,
  I am lord of the fowl and the brute.
O Solitude! where are the charms
  That sages have seen in thy face?
Better dwell in the midst of alarms,
  Than reign in this horrible place.

I am out of Humanity's reach,
  I must finish my journey alone,
Never hear the sweet music of speech,—
  I start at the sound of my own.
The beasts that roam over the plain,
  My form with indifference see,
They are so unacquainted with man,
  Their tameness is shocking to me.

Society, Friendship, and Love,
  Divinely bestowed upon man,
Oh! had I the wings of a dove,
  How soon would I taste you again!
My sorrows I then might assuage
  In the ways of religion and truth,
Might learn from the wisdom of age,
  And be cheered by the sallies of youth.

Religion! what treasure untold
   Resides in that heavenly word!
More precious than silver and gold,
   Or all that this earth can afford,
But the sound of the church-going bell
   These valleys and rocks never heard,
Ne'er sighed at the sound of a knell,
   Or smiled when the sabbath appeared.

Ye Winds that have made me your sport,
   Convey to this desolate shore,
Some cordial endearing report
   Of a land I shall visit no more.
My friends, do they now and then send
   A wish or a thought after me?
Oh! tell me I yet have a friend,
   Though a friend I am never to see.

How fleet is a glance of the Mind,
   Compared with the speed of its flight,
The Tempest itself lags behind,
   And the swift-wingèd arrows of Light.
When I think of my own native land,
   In a moment I seem to be there;
But alas! Recollection at hand
   Soon hurries me back to despair.

But the sea-fowl is gone to her nest,
   The beast is laid down in his lair,—
Even here is a season of rest,
   And I to my cabin repair.
There is Mercy in every place,
   And Mercy, encouraging thought!
Gives even Affliction a grace,
   And reconciles man to his lot.

The Castaway

Obscurest night involved the sky,
   The Atlantic billows roared,
When such a destined wretch as I,
   Washed headlong from on board,
Of friends, of hope, of all bereft,
His floating home for ever left.

No braver chief could Albion boast
   Than he with whom he went,
Nor ever ship left Albion's coast
   With warmer wishes sent.
He loved them both, but both in vain,
Nor him beheld, nor her again.

Not long beneath the whelming brine,
   Expert to swim, he lay;
Nor soon he felt his strength decline,
   Or courage die away:
But waged with Death a lasting strife,
Supported by despair of life.

He shouted; nor his friends had failed
   To check the vessel's course,
But so the furious blast prevailed,
   That, pitiless perforce,
They left their outcast mate behind,
And scudded still before the wind.

Some succour yet they could afford;
   And, such as storms allow,
The cask, the coop, the floated cord,
   Delayed not to bestow:
But he, they knew, nor ship, nor shore,
Whate'er they gave, should visit more.

Nor, cruel as it seemed, could he
   Their haste himself condemn,
Aware that flight, in such a sea,
   Alone could rescue them:
Yet bitter felt it still to die
Deserted, and his friends so nigh.

He long survives, who lives an hour
   In ocean, self-upheld:
And so long he, with unspent power,
   His destiny repelled:
And ever, as the minutes flew,
Entreated 'Help!' or cried—'Adieu!'

At length, his transient respite past,
   His comrades, who before
Had heard his voice in every blast,
   Could catch the sound no more:
For then, by toil subdued, he drank
The stifling wave, and then he sank.

No poet wept him; but the page
   Of narrative sincere,
That tells his name, his worth, his age,
   Is wet with Anson's tear:
And tears by bards or heroes shed
Alike immortalize the dead.

I therefore purpose not, or dream,
  Descanting on his fate,
To give the melancholy theme
  A more enduring date:
But misery still delights to trace
Its semblance in another's case.

No voice divine the storm allayed,
  No light propitious shone:
When, snatched from all effectual aid,
  We perished, each alone:
But I beneath a rougher sea
And whelmed in deeper gulfs than he.

To Mary

The twentieth year is well-nigh past,
Since first our sky was overcast;
Ah would that this might be the last!
     My Mary!

Thy spirits have a fainter flow,
I see thee daily weaker grow—
'Twas my distress that brought thee low,
     My Mary!

Thy needles, once a shining store,
For my sake restless heretofore,
Now rust disus'd, and shine no more,
     My Mary!

For though thou gladly wouldst fulfil
The same kind office for me still,
Thy sight now seconds not thy will,
     My Mary!

But well thou play'd'st the housewife's part,
And all thy threads with magic art
Have wound themselves about this heart,
     My Mary!

Thy indistinct expressions seem
Like language utter'd in a dream;
Yet me they charm, whate'er the theme,
     My Mary!

Thy silver locks, once auburn bright,
Are still more lovely in my sight
Than golden beams of orient light,
                    My Mary!

For could I view nor them nor thee,
What sight worth seeing could I see?
The sun would rise in vain for me,
                    My Mary!

Partakers of thy sad decline,
Thy hands their little force resign;
Yet, gently prest, press gently mine,
                    My Mary!

And then I feel that still I hold
A richer store ten thousandfold
Than misers fancy in their gold,
                    My Mary!

Such feebleness of limbs thou prov'st,
That now at every step thou mov'st
Upheld by two; yet still thou lov'st,
                    My Mary!

And still to love, though prest with ill,
In wintry age to feel no chill,
With me is to be lovely still,
                    My Mary!

But ah! by constant heed I know,
How oft the sadness that I show
Transforms thy smiles to looks of woe,
                    My Mary!

And should my future lot be cast
With much resemblance of the past,
Thy worn-out heart will break at last,
                    My Mary!

The Shrubbery

WRITTEN IN A TIME OF AFFLICTION

O happy shades!—to me unblest;
    Friendly to peace, but not to me;
How ill the scene that offers rest,
    And heart that cannot rest, agree!

This glassy stream, that spreading pine,
    Those alders quivering to the breeze,
Might soothe a soul less hurt than mine,
    And please, if any thing could please.

But fixed, unalterable care
    Foregoes not what she feels within,
Shows the same sadness every where,
    And slights the season and the scene.

For all that pleased in wood or lawn,
    While Peace possessed these silent bowers,
Her animating smile withdrawn,
    Has lost its beauties and its powers.

The saint or moralist should tread
    This moss-grown alley, musing, slow;
They seek like me the secret shade,
    But not like me to nourish woe!

Me fruitful scenes and prospects waste
    Alike admonish not to roam;
These tell me of enjoyments past,
    And those of sorrows yet to come.

The Poplar Field

The poplars are felled;—farewell to the shade,
And the whispering sound of the cool colonnade!
The winds play no longer and sing in the leaves,
Nor Ouse on his bosom their image receives.

Twelve years have elapsed since I first took a view
Of my favourite field, and the bank where they grew;
And now in the grass behold they are laid,
And the tree is my seat, that once lent me a shade.

The blackbird has fled to another retreat,
Where the hazels afford him a screen from the heat,
And the scene where his melody charmed me before,
Resounds with his sweet-flowing ditty no more.

My fugitive years are all hasting away,
And I must ere long lie as lowly as they,
With a turf on my breast, and a stone at my head,
Ere another such grove shall arise in its stead.

'Tis a sight to engage me, if any thing can,
To muse on the perishing pleasures of man;
Though his life be a dream, his enjoyments, I see,
Have a being less durable even than he.

Yardley Oak

Survivor sole, and hardly such, of all
That once lived here thy brethren! At my birth
(Since which I number threescore winters past),
A shattered veteran, hollow-trunked perhaps,
As now, and with excoriate forks deform,
Relics of ages! Could a mind, imbued
With truth from heaven, created thing adore,
I might with reverence kneel, and worship thee.
  It seems idolatry with some excuse,
When our forefather Druids in their oaks
Imagined sanctity. The conscience, yet
Unpurified by an authentic act
Of amnesty, the meed of blood divine,
Loved not the light, but gloomy, into gloom
Of thickest shades, like Adam after taste
Of fruit proscribed, as to a refuge, fled.
  Thou wast a bauble once, a cup and ball
Which babes might play with; and the thievish jay,
Seeking her food, with ease might have purloined
The auburn nut that held thee, swallowing down
Thy yet close-folded latitude of boughs,
And all thine embryo vastness, at a gulp.
But Fate thy growth decreed; autumnal rains
Beneath thy parent tree mellowed the soil
Designed thy cradle; and a skipping deer,
With pointed hoof dibbling the glebe, prepared
The soft receptacle, in which, secure,
Thy rudiments should sleep the winter through.
  So Fancy dreams. Disprove it, if ye can,

Ye reasoners broad awake, whose busy search
Of argument, employed too oft amiss,
Sifts half the pleasures of short life away!
    Thou fellest mature; and, in the loamy clod,
Swelling with vegetative force instinct,
Didst burst thine egg, as theirs the fabled twins,
Now stars; two lobes, protruding, paired exact;
A leaf succeeded, and another leaf,
And, all the elements thy puny growth
Fostering propitious, thou becamest a twig.
    Who lived when thou wast such? Oh, couldst thou
        speak,
As in Dodona once thy kindred trees
Oracular, I would not curious ask
The future, best unknown, but, at thy mouth
Inquisitive, the less ambiguous past.
    By thee I might correct, erroneous oft,
The clock of history, facts and events
Timing more punctual, unrecorded facts
Recovering, and misstated setting right—
Desperate attempt, till trees shall speak again!
    Time made thee what thou wast, king of the woods;
And Time hath made thee what thou art—a cave
For owls to roost in. Once thy spreading boughs
O'erhung the champaign; and the numerous flock
That grazed it stood beneath that ample cope
Uncrowded, yet safe sheltered from the storm.
No flock frequents thee now. Thou hast outlived
Thy popularity, and art become
(Unless verse rescues thee awhile) a thing
Forgotten, as the foliage of thy youth.
    While thus through all the stages thou hast pushed
Of treeship—first a seedling, hid in grass;
Then twig; then sapling; and, as century rolled
Slow after century, a giant bulk

68

Of girth enormous, with moss-cushioned root
Upheaved above the soil, and sides embossed
With prominent wens globose; till at the last
The rottenness, which time is charged to inflict
On other mighty ones, found also thee—
   What exhibitions various hath the world
Witnessed, of mutability in all
That we account most durable below!
Change is the diet on which all subsist,
Created changeable, and change at last
Destroys them—skies uncertain, now the heat
Transmitting cloudless, and the solar beam
Now quenching in a boundless sea of clouds—
Calm and alternate storm, moisture, and drought,
Invigorate by turns the springs of life
In all that live, plant, animal, and man,
And in conclusion mar them. Nature's threads,
Fine passing thought, e'en in her coarsest works,
Delight in agitation, yet sustain
The force that agitates not unimpaired;
But worn by frequent impulse, to the cause
Of their best tone their dissolution owe.
   Thought cannot spend itself, comparing still
The great and little of thy lot, thy growth
From almost nullity into a state
Of matchless grandeur, and declension thence,
Slow, into such magnificent decay.
Time was when, settling on thy leaf, a fly
Could shake thee to the root—and time has been
When tempests could not. At thy firmest age
Thou hadst within thy bole solid contents
That might have ribbed the sides or planked the deck
Of some flagged admiral; and tortuous arms,
The shipwright's darling treasure, didst present
To the four-quartered winds, robust and bold,

Warped into tough knee-timber, many a load!
But the axe spared thee. In those thriftier days
Oaks fell not, hewn by thousands, to supply
The bottomless demands of contest waged
For senatorial honours. Thus to Time
The task was left to whittle thee away
With his sly scythe, whose ever-nibbling edge,
Noiseless, an atom, and an atom more,
Disjoining from the rest, has, unobserved,
Achieved a labour which had, far and wide,
By man performed, made all the forest ring.
    Embowelled now, and of thy ancient self
Possessing naught but the scooped rind that seems
A huge throat calling to the clouds for drink,
Which it would give in rivulets to thy root,
Thou temptest none, but rather much forbiddest
The feller's toil which thou couldst ill requite.
Yet is thy root sincere, sound as the rock,
A quarry of stout spurs and knotted fangs,
Which, crooked into a thousand whimsies, clasp
The stubborn soil, and hold thee still erect.
    So stands a kingdom, whose foundations yet
Fail not, in virtue and in wisdom laid,
Though all the superstructure, by the tooth
Pulverized of venality, a shell
Stands now, and semblance only of itself!
    Thine arms have left thee. Winds have rent them off
Long since, and rovers of the forest wild
With bow and shaft have burnt them. Some have left
A splintered stump bleached to a snowy white;
And some memorial none where once they grew.
Yet Life still lingers in thee, and puts forth
Proof not contemptible of what she can,
Even where Death predominates. The spring
Thee finds not less alive to her sweet force

Than yonder upstarts of the neighbour wood,
So much thy juniors, who, their birth received
Half a millennium since the date of thine.
   But since, although well qualified by age
To teach, no Spirit dwells in thee, nor voice
May be expected from thee, seated here
On thy distorted root, with hearers none,
Or prompter, save the scene, I will perform
Myself the oracle, and will discourse
In my own ear such matter as I may.
   Thou, like myself, hast stage by stage attained
Life's wintry bourn; thou, after many years,
I after few; but few or many prove
A span in retrospect; for I can touch
With my least finger's end my own decease
And with extended thumb my natal hour,
And hadst thou also skill in measurement
As I, the past would seem as short to thee.
Evil and few—said Jacob—at an age
Thrice mine, and few and evil, I may think
The Prediluvian race, whose buxom youth
Endured two centuries, accounted theirs.
'Shortlived as foliage is the race of man.
The wind shakes down the leaves, the budding grove
Soon teems with others, and in spring they grow.
So pass mankind. One generation meets
Its destined period, and a new succeeds.'
Such was the tender but undue complaint
Of the Mæonian in old time; for who
Would drawl out centuries in tedious strife
Severe with mental and corporeal ill
And would not rather choose a shorter race
To glory, a few decades here below?
One man alone, the father of us all,
Drew not his life from woman; never gazed,

71

With mute unconsciousness of what he saw,
On all around him; learned not by degrees,
Nor owed articulation to his ear;
But moulded by his Maker into man
At once, upstood intelligent, surveyed
All creatures, with precision understood
Their purport, uses, properties, assigned
To each his name significant, and, filled
With love and wisdom, rendered back to Heaven
In praise harmonious the first air he drew.
He was excused the penalties of dull
Minority. No tutor charged his hand
With the thought-tracing quill, or tasked his mind
With problems. History, not wanted yet,
Leaned on her elbow, watching Time, whose course
Eventful, should supply her with a theme; . . .

Extracts from
The Task

How oft upon yon Eminence our pace
Has slackened to a pause, and we have borne
The ruffling wind, scarce conscious that it blew,
While Admiration, feeding at the eye,
And still unsated, dwelt upon the scene.
Thence with what pleasure have we just discerned
The distant plough slow-moving, and beside
His labouring team that swerved not from the track,
The sturdy swain diminished to a boy!
Here Ouse, slow-winding through a level plain
Of spacious meads with cattle sprinkled o'er,
Conducts the eye along his sinuous course
Delighted. There, fast rooted in their bank,
Stand, never overlooked, our favourite elms,
That screen the herdsman's solitary hut;
While far beyond, and overthwart the stream,
That, as with molten glass, inlays the vale,
The sloping land recedes into the clouds;
Displaying, on its varied side, the grace
Of hedge-row beauties numberless, square tower,
Tall spire, from which the sound of cheerful bells
Just undulates upon the listening ear,
Groves, heaths, and smoking villages, remote.
Scenes must be beautiful which, daily viewed,
Please daily, and whose novelty survives
Long knowledge and the scrutiny of years.
Praise justly due to those that I describe.
  Nor rural sights alone, but rural sounds,

Exhilarate the spirit, and restore
The tone of languid Nature. Mighty winds,
That sweep the skirt of some far-spreading wood
Of ancient growth, make music not unlike
The dash of Ocean on his winding shore,
And lull the spirit while they fill the mind,
Unnumbered branches waving in the blast,
And all their leaves fast fluttering, all at once.
Nor less composure waits upon the roar
Of distant floods, or on the softer voice
Of neighbouring fountain, or of rills that slip
Through the cleft rock, and, chiming as they fall
Upon loose pebbles, lose themselves at length
In matted grass, that with a livelier green
Betrays the secret of their silent course.
Nature inanimate employs sweet sounds,
But animated Nature sweeter still,
To soothe and satisfy the human ear.
Ten thousand warblers cheer the day, and one
The livelong night: nor these alone, whose notes
Nice-fingered Art must emulate in vain,
But cawing rooks, and kites that swim sublime
In still repeated circles, screaming loud,
The jay, the pie, and even the boding owl
That hails the rising moon, have charms for me.
Sounds inharmonious in themselves and harsh,
Yet heard in scenes where peace for ever reigns,
And only there, please highly for their sake.

From BOOK I

                              The sheepfold here
Pours out its fleecy tenants o'er the glebe.
At first, progressive as a stream, they seek
The middle field; but, scattered by degrees,

74

Each to his choice, soon whiten all the land.
There from the sunburnt hayfield homeward creeps
The loaded wain, while, lightened of its charge,
The wain that meets it passes swiftly by,
The boorish driver leaning o'er his team
Vociferous, and impatient of delay.
Nor less attractive is the woodland scene,
Diversified with trees of every growth,
Alike yet various. Here the grey smooth trunks
Of ash, or lime, or beech, distinctly shine,
Within the twilight of their distant shades;
There, lost behind a rising ground, the wood
Seems sunk, and shortened to its topmost boughs.
No tree in all the grove, but has its charms,
Though each its hue peculiar; paler some,
And of a wannish grey; the willow such,
And poplar that with silver lines his leaf,
And ash far-stretching his umbrageous arm;
Of deeper green the elm; and deeper still,
Lord of the woods, the long-surviving oak.
Some glossy-leaved, and shining in the sun,
The maple, and the beech of oily nuts
Prolific, and the lime at dewy eve
Diffusing odours: nor unnoted pass
The sycamore, capricious in attire,
Now green, now tawny, and, ere autumn yet
Have changed the woods, in scarlet honours bright.

From BOOK I

Ye fallen avenues! once more I mourn
Your fate unmerited, once more rejoice
That yet a remnant of your race survives.
How airy and how light the graceful arch,
Yet awful as the consecrated roof

Re-echoing pious anthems! while beneath
The chequer'd earth seems restless as a flood
Brush'd by the wind. So sportive is the light
Shot through the boughs, it dances as they dance,
Shadow and sunshine intermingling quick,
And dark'ning and enlight'ning, as the leaves
Play wanton, ev'ry moment, ev'ry spot.
And now, with nerves new-brac'd and spirits cheer'd,
We tread the wilderness, whose well-roll'd walks,
With curvature of slow and easy sweep—
Deception innocent—give ample space
To narrow bounds. The grove receives us next;
Between the upright shafts of whose tall elms
We may discern the thresher at his task.
Thump after thump resounds the constant flail,
That seems to swing uncertain, and yet falls
Full on the destin'd ear. Wide flies the chaff.
The rustling straw sends up a frequent mist
Of atoms, sparkling in the noon-day beam.
Come hither, ye that press your beds of down
And sleep not: see him sweating o'er his bread
Before he eats it.—'Tis the primal curse,
But soften'd into mercy; made the pledge
Of cheerful days, and nights without a groan.

From BOOK I

Oh for a lodge in some vast wilderness,
Some boundless contiguity of shade,
Where rumour of oppression and deceit,
Of unsuccessful or successful war,
Might never reach me more! My ear is pained,
My soul is sick, with every day's report
Of wrong and outrage with which earth is filled.
There is no flesh in man's obdurate heart,

It does not feel for man. The natural bond
Of brotherhood is severed as the flax
That falls asunder at the touch of fire.
He finds his fellow guilty of a skin
Not coloured like his own, and, having power
To enforce the wrong, for such a worthy cause
Dooms and devotes him as his lawful prey.
Lands intersected by a narrow frith
Abhor each other. Mountains interposed
Make enemies of nations who had else
Like kindred drops been mingled into one.
Thus man devotes his brother, and destroys;
And worse than all, and most to be deplored,
As human nature's broadest, foulest blot,
Chains him, and tasks him, and exacts his sweat
With stripes, that Mercy, with a bleeding heart,
Weeps when she sees inflicted on a beast.
Then what is man? And what man, seeing this
And having human feelings, does not blush,
And hang his head, to think himself a man?
I would not have a slave to till my ground,
To carry me, to fan me while I sleep,
And tremble when I wake, for all the wealth
That sinews bought and sold have ever earned.
No: dear as freedom is, and in my heart's
Just estimation prized above all price,
I had much rather be myself the slave,
And wear the bonds, than fasten them on him.
We have no slaves at home:—Then why abroad?
And they themselves once ferried o'er the wave
That parts us, are emancipate and loosed.
Slaves cannot breathe in England; if their lungs
Receive our air, that moment they are free;
They touch our country, and their shackles fall.
That's noble, and bespeaks a nation proud

And jealous of the blessing. Spread it then,
And let it circulate through every vein
Of all your empire; that where Britain's power
Is felt, mankind may feel her mercy too.

From BOOK II

They love the country, and none else, who seek
For their own sake its silence and its shade.
Delights which who would leave, that has a heart
Susceptible of pity, or a mind
Cultur'd and capable of sober thought,
For all the savage din of the swift pack,
And clamours of the field?—Detested sport,
That owes its pleasures to another's pain;
That feeds upon the sobs and dying shrieks
Of harmless nature, dumb, but yet endu'd
With eloquence, that agonies inspire,
Of silent tears and heart-distending sighs!
Vain tears, alas, and sighs that never find
A corresponding tone in jovial souls!
Well—one at least is safe. One shelter'd hare
Has never heard the sanguinary yell
Of cruel man, exulting in her woes.
Innocent partner of my peaceful home,
Whom ten long years' experience of my care
Has made at last familiar; she has lost
Much of her vigilant instinctive dread,
Not needful here, beneath a roof like mine.
Yes—thou may'st eat thy bread, and lick the hand
That feeds thee; thou may'st frolic on the floor
At evening, and at night retire secure
To thy straw couch, and slumber unalarm'd;
For I have gain'd thy confidence, have pledg'd
All that is human in me to protect

Thine unsuspecting gratitude and love.
If I survive thee I will dig thy grave;
And, when I place thee in it, sighing, say,
I knew at least one hare that had a friend.

From BOOK III

    The morning finds the self-sequestered man
Fresh for his task, intend what task he may.
Whether inclement seasons recommend
His warm but simple home, where he enjoys,
With her who shares his pleasures and his heart,
Sweet converse, sipping calm the fragrant lymph
Which neatly she prepares; then to his book
Well-chosen, and not sullenly perused
In selfish silence, but imparted oft,
As aught occurs that she may smile to hear,
Or turn to nourishment, digested well.
Or if the garden with its many cares,
All well repaid, demand him, he attends
The welcome call, conscious how much the hand
Of lubbard Labour needs his watchful eye,
Oft loitering lazily if not o'erseen,
Or misapplying his unskilful strength.
Nor does he govern only, or direct,
But much performs himself. No works, indeed,
That ask robust, tough sinews, bred to toil,
Servile employ; but such as may amuse,
Not tire, demanding rather skill than force.
Proud of his well-spread walls, he views his trees,
That meet (no barren interval between)
With pleasure more than even their fruits afford,
Which, save himself who trains them, none can feel;
These, therefore, are his own peculiar charge,
No meaner hand may discipline the shoots,

None but his steel approach them. What is weak,
Distempered, or has lost prolific powers,
Impaired by age, his unrelenting hand
Dooms to the knife; nor does he spare the soft
And succulent, that feeds its giant growth,
But barren, at the expense of neighbouring twigs
Less ostentatious, and yet studded thick
With hopeful gems. The rest, no portion left
That may disgrace his art, or disappoint
Large expectation, he disposes neat
At measured distances, that air and sun
Admitted freely, may afford their aid,
And ventilate and warm the swelling buds.
Hence Summer has her riches, Autumn hence,
And hence even Winter fills his withered hand
With blushing fruits, and plenty not his own.
Fair recompense of labour well bestowed,
And wise precaution, which a clime so rude
Makes needful still; whose Spring is but the child
Of churlish Winter, in her forward moods
Discovering much the temper of her sire.
For oft, as if in her the stream of mild
Maternal nature had reversed its course,
She brings her infants forth with many smiles,
But, once delivered, kills them with a frown.
He, therefore, timely warned, himself supplies
Her want of care, screening and keeping warm
The plenteous bloom, that no rough blast may sweep
His garlands from the boughs. Again, as oft
As the sun peeps, and vernal airs breathe mild,
The fence withdrawn, he gives them every beam,
And spreads his hopes before the blaze of day.
    To raise the prickly and green-coated gourd,
So grateful to the palate, and when rare
So coveted, else base and disesteemed—

Food for the vulgar merely—is an art
That toiling ages have but just matured,
And at this moment unassayed in song.
Yet gnats have had, and frogs and mice, long since,
Their eulogy; those sang the Mantuan bard,
And these the Grecian, in ennobling strains;
And in thy numbers, Phillips, shines for aye
The solitary Shilling. Pardon then,
Ye sage dispensers of poetic fame,
The ambition of one meaner far, whose powers,
Presuming an attempt not less sublime,
Pant for the praise of dressing to the taste
Of critic appetite, no sordid fare,
A cucumber, while costly yet and scarce.

The stable yields a stercoraceous heap,
Impregnated with quick fermenting salts,
And potent to resist the freezing blast;
For ere the beech and elm have cast their leaf
Deciduous, when now November dark
Checks vegetation in the torpid plant
Exposed to his cold breath, the task begins.
Warily, therefore, and with prudent heed,
He seeks a favoured spot; that where he builds
The agglomerated pile, his frame may front
The sun's meridian disk, and at the back
Enjoy close shelter, wall, or reeds, or hedge
Impervious to the wind. First he bids spread
Dry fern or littered hay, that may imbibe
The ascending damps; then leisurely impose,
And lightly, shaking it with agile hand
From the full fork, the saturated straw.
What longest binds the closest, forms secure
The shapely side, that as it rises takes,
By just degrees, an overhanging breadth,
Sheltering the base with its projected eaves.

The uplifted frame, compact at every joint,
And overlaid with clear translucent glass,
He settles next upon the sloping mount,
Whose sharp declivity shoots off secure
From the dashed pane the deluge as it falls:
He shuts it close, and the first labour ends.
Thrice must the voluble and restless earth
Spin round upon her axle, ere the warmth,
Slow gathering in the midst, through the square mass
Diffused, attain the surface; when, behold!
A pestilent and most corrosive steam,
Like a gross fog Bœtian, rising fast,
And fast condensed upon the dewy sash,
Asks egress; which obtained, the overcharged
And drenched conservatory breathes abroad,
In volumes wheeling slow, the vapour dank,
And purified, rejoices to have lost
Its foul inhabitant. But to assuage
The impatient fervour which it first conceives
Within its reeking bosom, threatening death
To his young hopes, requires discreet delay.
Experience, slow preceptress, teaching oft
The way to glory by miscarriage foul,
Must prompt him, and admonish how to catch
The auspicious moment, when the tempered heat
Friendly to vital motion, may afford
Soft fomentation, and invite the seed.
The seed, selected wisely, plump, and smooth,
And glossy, he commits to pots of size
Diminutive, well filled with well-prepared
And fruitful soil, that has been treasured long,
And drunk no moisture from the dripping clouds.
These on the warm and genial earth that hides
The smoking manure, and o'erspreads it all,
He places lightly, and as time subdues

The rage of fermentation, plunges deep
In the soft medium, till they stand immersed.
Then rise the tender germs, upstarting quick,
And spreading wide their spongy lobes, at first
Pale, wan, and livid, but assuming soon,
If fanned by balmy and nutritious air,
Strained through the friendly mats, a vivid green.
Two leaves produced, two rough indented leaves,
Cautious he pinches from the second stalk
A pimple that portends a future sprout,
And interdicts its growth. Thence straight succeed
The branches, sturdy to his utmost wish,
Prolific all, and harbingers of more.
The crowded roots demand enlargement now,
And transplantation in an ampler space.
Indulged in what they wish, they soon suppply
Large foliage, overshadowing golden flowers,
Blown on the summit of the apparent fruit.
These have their sexes; and, when summer shines,
The bee transports the fertilizing meal
From flower to flower, and even the breathing air
Wafts the rich prize to its appointed use.
Not so when winter scowls. Assistant Art
Then acts in Nature's office, brings to pass
The glad espousals, and ensures the crop.

From BOOK III

Hark! 'tis the twanging horn o'er yonder bridge,
That with its wearisome but needful length
Bestrides the wintry flood, in which the moon
Sees her unwrinkled face reflected bright;—
He comes, the herald of a noisy world,
With spattered boots, strapped waist, and frozen locks,
News from all nations lumbering at his back.

True to this charge, the close-packed load behind,
Yet careless what he brings, his one concern
Is to conduct it to the destined inn,
And, having dropped the expected bag, pass on.
He whistles as he goes, light-hearted wretch,
Cold and yet cheerful; messenger of grief
Perhaps to thousands, and of joy to some;
To him indifferent whether grief or joy.
Houses in ashes, and the fall of stocks,
Births, deaths, and marriages, epistles wet
With tears that trickled down the writer's cheeks
Fast as the periods from his fluent quill,
Or charged with amorous signs of absent swains,
Or nymphs responsive, equally affect
His horse and him, unconscious of them all.
But oh the important budget! ushered in
With such heart-shaking music, who can say
What are its tidings? Have our troops awaked?
Or do they still, as if with opium drugged,
Snore to the murmurs of the Atlantic wave?
Is India free? And does she wear her plumed
And jewelled turban with a smile of peace?
Or do we grind her still? The grand debate,
The popular harangue, the tart reply,
The logic, and the wisdom, and the wit,
And the loud laugh—I long to know them all;
I burn to set the imprisoned wranglers free,
And give them voice and utterance once again.
    Now stir the fire, and close the shutters fast,
Let fall the curtains, wheel the sofa round,
And while the bubbling and loud-hissing urn
Throws up a steamy column, and the cups
That cheer but not inebriate, wait on each,
So let us welcome peaceful evening in.

From BOOK IV

Just when our drawing-rooms begin to blaze
With lights, by clear reflection multiplied
From many a mirror, in which he of Gath,
Goliath, might have seen his giant bulk
Whole without stooping, towering crest and all,
My pleasures too begin. But me, perhaps,
The glowing hearth may satisfy awhile
With faint illumination, that uplifts
The shadow to the ceiling, there by fits
Dancing uncouthly to the quivering flame.
Not undelightful is an hour to me
So spent in parlour twilight; such a gloom
Suits well the thoughtful, or unthinking mind,
The mind contemplative, with some new theme
Pregnant, or indisposed alike to all.
Laugh ye, who boast your more mercurial powers
That never felt a stupor, know no pause,
Nor need one; I am conscious and confess,
Fearless, a soul that does not always think.
Me oft has Fancy, ludicrous and wild,
Soothed with a waking dream of houses, towers,
Trees, churches, and strange visages, expressed
In the red cinders, while with poring eye
I gazed, myself creating what I saw.
Nor less amused, have I quiescent watched
The sooty films that play upon the bars,
Pendulous, and foreboding, in the view
Of superstition, prophesying still,
Though still deceived, some stranger's near approach.
'Tis thus the understanding takes repose
In indolent vacuity of thought,
And sleeps and is refreshed. Meanwhile the face
Conceals the mood lethargic with a mask
Of deep deliberation, as the man
Were tasked to his full strength, absorbed and lost.

Thus oft, reclined at ease, I lose an hour
At evening, till at length the freezing blast,
That sweeps the bolted shutter, summons home
The recollected powers, and snapping short
The glassy threads with which the Fancy weaves
Her brittle toys, restores me to myself.
How calm is my recess, and how the frost,
Raging abroad, and the rough wind, endear
The silence and the warmth enjoyed within.
I saw the woods and fields at close of day
A variegated show; the meadows green
Though faded; and the lands where lately waved
The golden harvest, of a mellow brown,
Upturned so lately by the forceful share.
I saw far off the weedy fallows smile
With verdure not unprofitable, grazed
By flocks, fast feeding and selecting each
His favourite herb; while all the leafless groves
That skirt the horizon, wore a sable hue,
Scarce noticed in the kindred dusk of eve.
To-morrow brings a change, a total change!
Which even now, though silently performed
And slowly, and by most unfelt, the face
Of universal nature undergoes.
Fast falls a fleecy shower: the downy flakes
Descending, and with never-ceasing lapse
Softly alighting upon all below,
Assimilate all objects. Earth receives
Gladly the thickening mantle, and the green
And tender blade, that feared the chilling blast,
Escapes unhurt beneath so warm a veil.
   In such a world, so thorny, and where none
Finds happiness unblighted, or if found,
Without some thistly sorrow at its side,
It seems the part of wisdom, and no sin

Against the law of love, to measure lots
With less distinguished than ourselves, that thus
We may with patience bear our moderate ills,
And sympathise with others suffering more.
Ill fares the traveller now, and he that stalks
In ponderous boots beside his reeking team.
The wain goes heavily, impeded sore
By congregated loads adhering close
To the clogged wheels; and in its sluggish pace
Noiseless, appears a moving hill of snow.
The toiling steeds expand the nostril wide,
While every breath, by respiration strong
Forced downwards, is consolidated soon
Upon their jutting chests. He, formed to bear
The pelting brunt of the tempestuous night,
With half-shut eyes, and puckered cheeks, and teeth
Presented bare against the storm, plods on.
One hand secures his hat, save when with both
He brandishes his pliant length of whip,
Resounding oft, and never heard in vain.
O happy! and, in my account, denied
That sensibility of pain with which
Refinement is endued, thrice happy thou!
Thy frame, robust and hardy, feels indeed
The piercing cold, but feels it unimpaired.
The learned finger never need explore
Thy vigorous pulse, and the unhealthful East,
That breathes the spleen, and searches every bone
Of the infirm, is wholesome air to thee.
Thy days roll on exempt from household care;
Thy waggon is thy wife, and the poor beasts
That drag the dull companion to and fro,
Thine helpless charge, dependent on thy care.
Ah, treat them kindly! rude as thou appearest,
Yet show that thou hast mercy, which the great,

With needless hurry whirled from place to place,
Humane as they would seem, not always show.

From BOOK IV

'Tis morning; and the sun, with ruddy orb
Ascending, fires the horizon; while the clouds
That crowd away before the driving wind,
More ardent as the disk emerges more,
Resemble most some city in a blaze,
Seen through the leafless wood. His slanting ray
Slides ineffectual down the snowy vale,
And, tinging all with his own rosy hue,
From every herb and every spiry blade
Stretches a length of shadow o'er the field.
Mine, spindling into longitude immense,
In spite of gravity, and sage remark
That I myself am but a fleeting shade,
Provokes me to a smile. With eye askance
I view the muscular proportioned limb
Transformed to a lean shank. The shapeless pair,
As they designed to mock me, at my side
Take step for step; and as I near approach
The cottage, walk along the plastered wall,
Preposterous sight! the legs without the man.
The verdure of the plain lies buried deep
Beneath the dazzling deluge; and the bents
And coarser grass, unspearing o'er the rest,
Of late unsightly and unseen, now shine
Conspicuous, and in bright apparel clad,
And fledged with icy feathers, nod superb.
The cattle mourn in corners where the fence
Screens them, and seem half petrified to sleep
In unrecumbent sadness. There they wait
Their wonted fodder, not like hungering man,

Fretful if unsupplied, but silent, meek,
And patient of the slow-paced swain's delay.
He from the stack carves out the accustomed load,
Deep-plunging and again deep-plunging oft,
His broad keen knife into the solid mass:
Smooth as a wall the upright remnant stands,
With such undeviating and even force
He severs it away: no needless care,
Lest storms should overset the leaning pile
Deciduous, or its own unbalanced weight.
  Forth goes the woodman, leaving unconcerned
The cheerful haunts of man, to wield the axe,
And drive the wedge in yonder forest drear,
From morn to eve his solitary task.
Shaggy and lean, and shrewd, with pointed ears
And tail cropped short, half lurcher and half cur,
His dog attends him. Close behind his heel
Now creeps he slow; and now, with many a frisk
Wide scampering, snatches up the drifted snow
With ivory teeth, or ploughs it with his snout;
Then shakes his powdered coat, and barks for joy.
Heedless of all his pranks, the sturdy churl
Moves right toward the mark; nor stops for aught,
But, now and then, with pressure of his thumb
To adjust the fragrant charge of a short tube,
That fumes beneath his nose: the trailing cloud
Streams far behind him, scenting all the air.
Now from the roost, or from the neighbouring pale,
Where diligent to catch the first faint gleam
Of smiling day, they gossiped side by side,
Come trooping at the housewife's well-known call
The feathered tribes domestic. Half on wing
And half on foot, they brush the fleecy flood,
Conscious, and fearful of too deep a plunge.
The sparrows peep, and quit the sheltering eaves,

To seize the fair occasion. Well they eye
The scattered grain, and thievishly resolved
To escape the impending famine, often scared
As oft return, a pert voracious kind.
Clean riddance quickly made, one only care
Remains to each, the search of sunny nook,
Or shed impervious to the blast. Resigned
To sad necessity, the cock foregoes
His wonted strut, and wading at their head
With well-considered steps, seems to resent
His altered gait and stateliness retrenched.
How find the myriads, that in summer cheer
The hills and valleys with their ceaseless songs,
Due sustenance, or where subsist they now?
Earth yields them naught: the imprisoned worm is safe
Beneath the frozen clod; all seeds of herbs
Lie covered close; and berry-bearing thorns
That feed the thrush (whatever some suppose)
Afford the smaller minstrels no supply.
The long protracted rigour of the year
Thins all their numerous flocks. In chinks and holes
Ten thousand seek an unmolested end,
As instinct prompts; self-buried ere they die.
The very rooks and daws forsake the fields,
Where neither grub, nor root, nor earth-nut, now
Repays their labour more; and perched aloft
By the wayside, or stalking in the path,
Lean pensioners upon the traveller's track,
Pick up their nauseous dole, though sweet to them,
Of voided pulse or half-digested grain.
The streams are lost amid the splendid blank,
O'erwhelming all distinction. On the flood,
Indurated and fixed, the snowy weight
Lies undissolved; while silently beneath,
And unperceived, the current steals away.

Not so, where, scornful of a check, it leaps
The mill-dam, dashes on the restless wheel,
And wantons in the pebbly gulf below:
No frost can bind it there; its utmost force
Can but arrest the light and smoky mist
That in its fall the liquid sheet throws wide.
And see where it has hung the embroidered banks
With forms so various, that no powers of art,
The pencil, or the pen, may trace the scene!
Here glittering turrets rise, upbearing high
(Fantastic misarrangement!) on the roof
Large growth of what may seem the sparkling trees
And shrubs of fairy land. The crystal drops
That trickle down the branches, fast congealed,
Shoot into pillars of pellucid length,
And prop the pile they but adorned before.
Here grotto within grotto safe defies
The sunbeam; there embossed and fretted wild,
The growing wonder takes a thousand shapes
Capricious, in which Fancy seeks in vain
The likeness of some object seen before.

From BOOK V

The night was winter in his roughest mood;
The morning sharp and clear. But now at noon
Upon the southern side of the slant hills,
And where the woods fence off the northern blast,
The season smiles, resigning all its rage,
And has the warmth of May. The vault is blue
Without a cloud, and white without a speck
The dazzling splendour of the scene below.
Again the harmony comes o'er the vale,
And through the trees I view the embattled tower
Whence all the music. I again perceive

The soothing influence of the wafted strains,
And settle in soft musings as I tread
The walk, still verdant under oaks and elms,
Whose outspread branches overarch the glade.
The roof, though moveable through all its length
As the wind sways it, has yet well sufficed,
And, intercepting in their silent fall
The frequent flakes, has kept a path for me.
No noise is here, or none that hinders thought.
The redbreast warbles still, but is content
With slender notes, and more than half suppressed:
Pleased with his solitude, and flitting light
From spray to spray, where'er he rests he shakes
From many a twig the pendent drops of ice,
That tinkle in the withered leaves below.
Stillness, accompanied with sounds so soft,
Charms more than silence. Meditation here
May think down hours to moments. Here the heart
May give an useful lesson to the head,
And Learning wiser grow without his books.
Knowledge and Wisdom, far from being one,
Have ofttimes no connexion. Knowledge dwells
In heads replete with thoughts of other men,
Wisdom in minds attentive to their own.
Knowledge, a rude unprofitable mass,
The mere materials with which Wisdom builds,
Till smoothed and squared and fitted to its place,
Does but encumber whom it seems to enrich.
Knowledge is proud that he has learned so much,
Wisdom is humble that he knows no more.
Books are not seldom talismans and spells,
By which the magic art of shrewder wits
Holds an unthinking multitude enthralled.
Some to the fascination of a name
Surrender judgment hoodwinked. Some the style

Infatuates, and through labyrinths and wilds
Of error, leads them by a tune entranced.
While sloth seduces more, too weak to bear
The insupportable fatigue of thought,
And swallowing, therefore, without pause or choice,
The total grist unsifted, husks and all.
But trees, and rivulets whose rapid course
Defies the check of winter, haunts of deer,
And sheepwalks populous with bleating lambs,
And lanes in which the primrose ere her time
Peeps through the moss that clothes the hawthorn root,
Deceive no student. Wisdom there, and Truth,
Not shy as in the world, and to be won
By slow solicitation, seize at once
The roving thought, and fix it on themselves.
    What prodigies can power divine perform
More grand than it produces year by year,
And all in sight of inattentive man?
Familiar with the effect we slight the cause,
And in the constancy of Nature's course,
The regular return of genial months,
And renovation of a faded world,
See naught to wonder at. Should God again,
As once in Gibeon, interrupt the race
Of the undeviating and punctual sun,
How would the world admire! But speaks it less
An agency divine, to make him know
His moment when to sink and when to rise,
Age after age, than to arrest his course?
All we behold is miracle, but seen
So duly, all is miracle in vain.
Where now the vital energy that moved,
While summer was, the pure and subtle lymph
Through the imperceptible meandering veins
Of leaf and flower? It sleeps; and the icy touch

Of unprolific winter has impressed
A cold stagnation on the intestine tide.
But let the months go round, a few short months,
And all shall be restored. These naked shoots,
Barren as lances, among which the wind
Makes wintry music, sighing as it goes,
Shall put their graceful foliage on again,
And more aspiring, and with ampler spread,
Shall boast new charms, and more than they have lost.
Then each in its peculiar honours clad,
Shall publish, even to the distant eye,
Its family and tribe. Laburnum, rich
In streaming gold; Syringa, ivory pure;
The scentless and the scented Rose, this red,
And of an humbler growth, the other* tall,
And throwing up into the darkest gloom
Of neighbouring Cypress, or more sable Yew,
Her silver globes, light as the foamy surf,
That the wind severs from the broken wave;
The Lilac, various in array, now white,
Now sanguine, and her beauteous head now set
With purple spikes pyramidal, as if
Studious of ornament, yet unresolved
Which hue she most approved, she chose them all;
Copious of flowers the Woodbine, pale and wan,
But well compensating her sickly looks
With never cloying odours, early and late;
Hypericum all bloom, so thick a swarm
Of flowers, like flies clothing her slender rods,
That scarce a leaf appears; Mezereon too,
Though leafless, well attired, and thick beset
With blushing wreaths, investing every spray;
Althæa with the purple eye; the Broom,

* The Guelder rose—(C.)

Yellow and bright, as bullion unalloyed,
Her blossoms; and luxuriant above all
The Jasmine, throwing wide her elegant sweets,
The deep dark green of whose unvarnished leaf
Makes more conspicuous, and illumines more
The bright confusion of her scattered stars.—
These have been, and these shall be in their day;
And all this uniform uncoloured scene
Shall be dismantled of its fleecy load,
And flush into variety again.
From dearth to plenty, and from death to life,
Is Nature's progress, when she lectures man
In heavenly truth; evincing as she makes
The grand transition, that there lives and works
A soul in all things, and that soul is God.
The beauties of the wilderness are his,
That makes so gay the solitary place,
Where no eye sees them. And the fairer forms
That cultivation glories in, are his.
He sets the bright procession on its way,
And marshals all the order of the year;
He marks the bounds which Winter may not pass,
And blunts his pointed fury; in its case,
Russet and rude, folds up the tender germ
Uninjured, with inimitable art;
And ere one flowery season fades and dies,
Designs the blooming wonders of the next.

From BOOK VI

Index of First Lines

(* denotes an extract from *The Task*)

A poet's cat, sedate and grave	*page* 36
Big with great purposes and proud they sat	29
Close by the threshold of a door nailed fast	34
Far from the world, O Lord, I flee	25
God moves in a mysterious way	26
*Hark! 'tis the twanging horn o'er yonder bridge	83
Here lies, whom hound did ne'er pursue	30
*How oft upon yon Eminence our pace	73
I am monarch of all I survey	57
It happened on a solemn eventide	27
Jesus, where'er thy people meet	24
John Gilpin was a citizen	45
*Just when our drawing-rooms begin to blaze	85
O happy shades!—to me unblest	65
Obscurest night involved the sky	59
Oh! for a closer walk with God	23
*Oh for a lodge in some vast wilderness	76
Oh that those lips had language! Life has passed	19
Survivor sole, and hardly such, of all	67
*The morning finds the self-sequestered man	79
*The night was winter in his roughest mood	91
The poplars are felled;—farewell to the shade	66
*The sheepfold here	74
The twentieth year is well-nigh past	62
There is a field through which I often pass	40
*They love the country, and none else, who seek	78
*'Tis morning; and the sun, with ruddy orb	88
To grass, or leaf, or fruit, or wall	32
When a bar of pure silver or ingot of gold	56
Whence is it, that amaz'd I hear	33
*Ye fallen avenues! once more I mourn	75
Yon ancient prude, whose withered features show	55